The Shortcut!
Companion Workbook

The fastest route to selling your services better than you ever have before so that you earn more money than you ever have before!

Brian K. McNeill

Very Personal Sales Coaching

ISBN-10: 1534979417
ISBN-13: 978-1534979413

About Brian K. McNeill

Brian K. McNeill is a sales coach, speaker, author, workshop facilitator and business owner. He teaches people who sell services how to sell their services better than ever before so that they can earn more money than they ever have before.

Brian K. McNeill is the founder of M.E.N. (Male Empowerment Networks) which is a discussion group for men and young men in the Charlotte Area. He is a member of Toastmasters International™.

Block One

What do you do for a living?

Your Story

Ten to Win

Magic Numbers!

Block Two

How to get and stay profitable: The Selling Your Services Campaign

Drop me in Dubuque

Block Three

Why People Will Buy from You

Why People Will NOT Buy from You

The 4 Chances You Get to Overcome an Objection

5 Steps to Overcoming ANY Objection

Why You CANNOT Fail in Selling Your Services

Block One

What do you do for a living?

The scene: You are at a mixer/party (not a business event). You end up in a huddle with a couple of ladies, a couple of guys. Someone asks, "What do you do for a living?

You say: _____

_____

_____

_____

_____

(tell your story)

Your Story

You know how…

_____

_____

_____

Well, what I do is…

_____

_____

_____

So that they can…

_____

_____

_____

Ten to Win

Ten GREAT Reasons Why Someone Should Hire ME and MY Services

3 Minutes

1. _____
2. _____
3. _____
4. _____
5. _____
6. _____
7. _____
8. _____
9. _____
10. _____

Ten Characteristics of MY Ideal Client

3 Minutes

1. _____
2. _____
3. _____
4. _____
5. _____
6. _____
7. _____
8. _____
9. _____
10. _____

THE IDEAL CLIENT

Ten Characteristics of an OUTSTANDING _____

3 Minutes

1. _____
2. _____
3. _____
4. _____
5. _____
6. _____
7. _____
8. _____
9. _____
10. _____

Magic Numbers!

The Number Zero (0)

_____

The Number Two or Three (2 or 3)

_____

_____

The Number Four (4)

_____

_____

_____

The Number Five (5)

_____

_____

The Number One Hundred (100)

_____

_____

_____

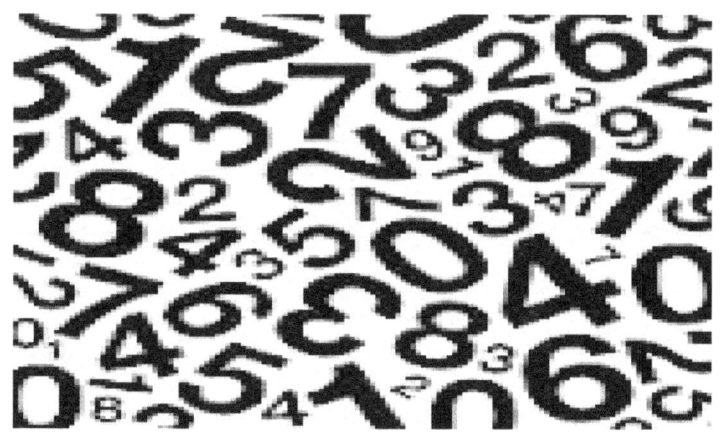

Notes

Block Two

How to get and stay profitable: The Selling Your Services Campaign

Step One: Identifying Targets

_____

_____

_____

Step Two: Initial Email (Touch One)

_____

_____

_____

Step Three: Initial Phone Call (Touch Two)

_____

_____

_____

Step Four: Second Email (Touch Three)

_____

_____

_____

Step Five: Second Phone Call (Touch Four)

_____

_____

_____

Step Six: To YOUR Comfort Level (Touch Five)
(Letter, Phone Call, Text, Email)

_____

_____

_____

Drop me in Dubuque

Game: I fly you into Dubuque, IA on Monday morning at 8am. You are checked into your hotel by 9am.

You have:

- No leads
- No contacts
- Don't know the area
- No one knows you

You are armed with only your cell phone, laptop and a rental car. The question is: In this scenario, can you make a sale before close of business on Friday?

How:

_____

_____

_____

_____

_____

Notes

Block Three

7 Reasons Why People Historically Buy

1. _____
2. _____
3. _____
4. _____
5. _____
6. _____
7. _____

5 Reasons Why People Will Not Buy From You

1. _____
2. _____
3. _____
4. _____
5. _____

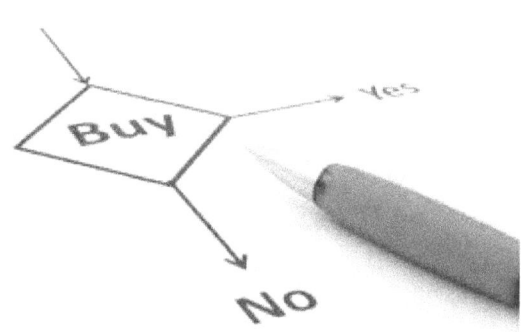

Emotional Selling vs Logical Selling

_____

_____

_____

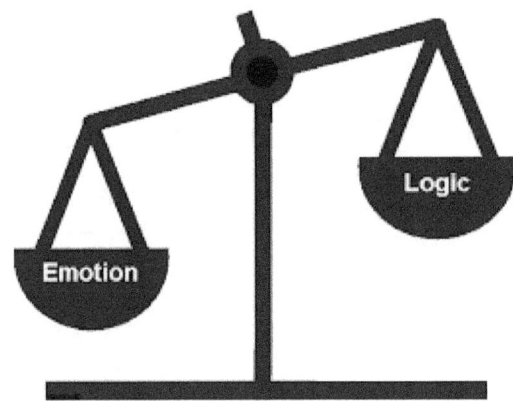

How to use Voice inflection to persuade

_____

_____

_____

The 4 Chances You Get to Overcome an Objection

1. _____
2. _____
3. _____
4. _____

5 Steps to Overcoming ANY Objection

1. _____
2. _____
3. _____
4. _____
5. _____

The two essential closes

1. _____
   _____
   _____

2. _____
   _____
   _____

Why You CANNOT Fail in Selling Your Services

_____

_____

_____

_____

YOU CANNOT FAIL

Notes

_____

_____

_____

_____

_____

_____

_____

_____

_____

_____

_____

_____

_____

_____

Notes

Notes

_____

_____

_____

_____

_____

_____

_____

_____

_____

_____

_____

_____

_____

_____

Notes

Notes

_____

_____

_____

_____

_____

_____

_____

_____

_____

_____

_____

_____

_____

_____

_____

_____

_____

_____

Brian K McNeill

Sales Coach, Author, Professional Speaker, Workshop Facilitator and Founder of M.E.N (male empowerment networks) of Charlotte and of Greensboro NC, Sales Coordinator of the Empowerment Center of Charlotte.

For over 24 years Brian has been engaged in the act and art of helping other people to Sell themselves and their Services better than they ever have before so that they earn more money than they ever have before.

For the first 12 of these 24 years Brian was the sales manager of a multistate Home improvement company with 17 offices. It was during those years of giving 5 motivational sales meetings a week that Brian honed his skills in selling and teaching sales.

In 1996 Brian wrote "The 22 Must Closes" 22 ways that salespeople should know how to ask for money. That publication launched Brian as an authority. Thousands of men and women have been wonderfully and powerfully impacted for the rest of their lives by what they have learned from Brian.

In 2006 Brian Launched his own Sales Training Company as "Rhino Sales and Seminars" and it was in those years from 2006 to 2010 That Brian discovered the secret as to why sales training did not seem to last as long as he would like. The secret is in the personalization of the training and coaching, so in 2010 Brian re-launched his company as Very Personal Sales Coaching.

It is Brian's strong belief that most sales training is ineffective because it is not personalized enough.

Since 2010 thousands have been helped to Sell much better than they ever have before and Brian's Signature workshop "Ten to Win" has been requested over and over and over again.

As more than 200 written testimonials of Brian's effectiveness can attest, he can help you to Sell your services much better than you ever have before.

Brian's work has always been motivational and inspirational in nature so he has willingly shared many motivational messages in schools, churches, and corporate functions.

Brian is the founder of the M.E.N (male empowerment networks) organization. M.E.N is a time and place where men and teenaged men can get together and be transparent and helpful to each other.

Look for Brian's other books "Asking for the Money" the very best of old school and new school methods of closing the sale and his children's book "Why Rhinos make great Salespeople" featuring Mr. Randall the Rhino.

Brian currently lives in Charlotte NC with his wife Lisa Santiago McNeill

Brian K McNeill
919 345 4893
Very Personal Sales Coaching
http://www.verypersonalsalescoaching.com
brian@verypersonalsalescoaching.com
https://www.linkedin.com/in/themostfunspeaker
https://www.facebook.com/brian.k.mcneill
https://twitter.com/BrianKMcNeill